Texas Bucket List Adventure Guide & Journal

Explore 50 Natural Wonders You Must See!

Bridge Press

Bridge Press
dp@purplelink.org

Please consider writing a review!
Just visit: purplelink.org/review

ISBN: 978-1-955149-19-8

FREE BONUS

Find Out 31 Incredible Places You Can Visit Next! Just Go To:

purplelink.org/travel

Table of Contents:

How to Use This Book

Welcome to your very own adventure guide to exploring the natural wonders of the state of Texas. Not only does this book lay out the most wonderful places to visit and sights to see in this vast state, but it also serves as a journal so that you can record your experiences.

Adventure Guide
Sorted by region, this guide highlights 50 amazing wonders of nature found in Texas for you to go see and explore. These can be visited in any order, and this book will help keep track of where you've been and where to look forward to next.

Each section describes the area or place, what to look for, how to get there, and what you may need to bring along. A map is also included so that you can plot your destinations.

Document Your Experiences
There is a blank journal page after each location description to help you record your experiences. During or after your visit, you can jot down significant sights you encountered, events that occurred, people involved, and memories you gained while on your adventure. This will add even more value to your experience and maintain a record of your time spent witnessing the greatest wonders of Texas.

GPS Coordinates and Codes
As you can imagine, not all of the locations in this book have a physical address. Fortunately, some of our listed wonders are either located within a national park or reserve, or are near a city, town, or place of business. For those that are not associated with a specific location, it is easiest to map it using GPS coordinates.

Luckily, Google has a system of codes that converts the coordinates into pin drop locations that Google Maps is able to interpret and navigate.

Each adventure in this guide will include GPS coordinates, general directions on how to find the location, and Google Plus codes whenever possible.

How to find a location using Google Plus:

1. Open Google Maps on your device.
2. In the search bar, type the Google Plus code as it is printed on the page.
3. Once the pin is located, you can tap on "Directions" for step-by-step navigation.

It's important that you are prepared for poor cell signal. It's a good practice to route your location and ensure that directions are accessible offline as well. Depending on your device and the distance of some locations, you may need to travel with a backup battery source.

About Texas

Texas is the biggest state in the continental United States, second only to Alaska overall. It's located in the American Southwest and spans over 265,000 square miles. Twenty-nine million people call this state home. It features some of the nation's most notable cities such as Houston, Dallas, El Paso, San Antonio, and Austin.

Texas became the twenty-eighth state on December 29, 1845. This was ten years after gaining its independence from Mexico. For that decade, Texas was its own nation, which is why you'll find a lot of Texas pride around the state. It's the only state in the country that was once a separate nation of its own.

Known as the *Lone Star State*, the state flag is the adopted flag of independence from Mexico. It symbolizes the independent spirit of Texans.

Texas is also known for its vibrant mix of cultures. Whether you're going for a stroll on San Antonio's Riverwalk or hiking the backwoods of Big Bend, Texas has a little bit of everything for everyone. In fact, Houston prides itself as the most diverse city in the country.

Because Texas used to belong to Mexico, there is a strong presence of Mexican culture and tradition. From statewide Dia de los Muertos celebrations to family fajita BBQs on weekend afternoons, Texans love to celebrate their rich cultural history.

It's also impossible to mention Texas without mentioning one of the state's treasures: Willie Nelson. Originally born in Texas's Hill Country, Willie Nelson has been a mascot and advocate of all things Texas for the entirety of his career. He's a beloved figure in the great state.

Texas is home to beaches, swimming holes, mountains, deserts, swamplands, plains, and tropics. Its vastness is quite remarkable. The number of things to do in Texas is endless. There are museums and natural wonders all throughout the state as well.

A state that was once known for its oil and gas industry, Texas is now moving towards a bigger technology industry. People from around the country are moving to cities like Houston and Austin for the opportunities and excitement those regions offer.

Even though there's a lot of tech growth in the state, it still boasts plenty of open spaces. When driving through West Texas, you'll feel like you were plucked out of present-day life and thrown into an old Western film with its sprawling red mountains and tumbleweeds on dirt roads. Texas's natural landscape is as diverse as its people.

Landscape and Climate

Texas's landscape and climate are both wide-ranging. Its weather and natural scenery vary greatly from east to west and north to south. Texas is a huge state that covers a lot of land, boasting over 350 miles of shoreline along the Gulf of Mexico.

Folks from out of state tend to think of Texas as a dry, hot desert, but Texas is actually home to three different types of climates. Each region has a unique landscape that contributes to the weather.

The northern panhandle is known as the "Texas High Plains." This area experiences extreme temperature ranges, low humidity, and little rainfall. It's known for its flat land, hot summers, and mild winters.

Central and coastal Texas is known for more humid weather, as it's closer to the Texas Gulf shoreline. It experiences colder winters and much hotter and more humid summers.

Finally, West Texas features the dry, desert mountains that the state is known for.

4

Map of Texas

Big Bend National Park

Big Bend National Park is one of the most beautiful places to travel in Texas. During the day, the red Chisos Mountains sprawl high and tall against a beautiful blue sky. At night, the stars illuminate a history and culture that is both sacred and simple.

Big Bend sits along the Rio Grande River and shares a border with Mexico to its south. The park is home to the entire Chisos Mountain Range and a large portion of the Chihuahuan Desert.

Best time to visit:
It's best to plan a trip to Big Bend National Park either in the milder spring or fall weather. Winter and summer temperatures tend to be extreme and pose challenges for campers and visitors.

Pass/Permit/Fees:
No reservations required. Park visitors are required to purchase a recreational pass. Fees vary depending on vehicle, group size, and desired camping accommodations.

Closest city or town:
Terlingua

How to get there:
The distance between towns is significant. Be sure to have enough gas, oil, and food to make the trip.

TX 118 from Alpine to Study Butte
FM 170 from Presidio to Study Butte

GPS coordinates:
29.2498° N, 103.2502° W

Did you know?
Big Bend National Park is home to over 450 species of birds.

Journal:

Date(s) Visited:

Weather
conditions:

Who you were with:

Nature observations:

Special memories:

Palo Duro Canyon

If natural beauty millions of years old is your thing, Palo Duro
Canyon State Park is a must visit in Texas. Perfect for day trips,
overnight camping trips, or extended stays, this state park is located
in the northern part of the Texas Panhandle. It's by far one of the
most beautiful and scenic places to visit in that area.

The park was formed as a result of millions of years of erosion
from the Red River and West Texas wind. It offers incredible
views, scenic drives, picnic areas, historical sites, markets, and
miles of hiking opportunities. And what would a Texas state park
be without horseback riding as well?

Best time to visit:
Spring or late fall. Summers in the canyon can get hot, so if you do
visit at that time, it's recommended to go early in the morning.

Pass/Permit/Fees:
Children under 12 are free. Adults are $8.

Closest city or town:
Amarillo

How to get there:
From the north: south on I27 and east on TX-217
From the south: north on I27 and east on TX-217
From the west: east on US-60 to TX-217
From the east: north on I27 and east on TX-217

GPS coordinates:
34.9373° N, 101.6589° W

Did you know?
There is a descent of 800 feet to the canyon floor.

Journal:

Date(s) Visited:

Weather
conditions:

Who you were with:

Nature observations:

Special memories:

Lady Bird Lake

Lady Bird Lake flows through downtown Austin and is the main attraction when traveling to the Texas capital. Although technically a reservoir, you can find many people hiking, biking, and gathering along and around the trail.

Originally created as a cooling spot for the downtown power plant, Lady Bird Lake has a surface area of 416 acres. The lake features many attractions such as boating, canoeing, paddle-boarding, evening cruises, bat-watching, and more. Lady Bird Lake offers 10 miles of surrounding trails with spectacular views of downtown Austin and its skyline.

Best time to visit:
Spring or fall

Pass/Permit/Fees:
No passes or permits needed.

Closest city or town:
Austin

How to get there:
From the north: South on I35 to Riverside Drive
From the south: North on I35 to Riverside Drive
From the east: West on US290 to South Congress
From the west: East on US290 to South Congress

GPS coordinates:
30.2477° N, 97.7181° W

Did you know?
The South Congress Bridge that crosses over Lady Bird Lake is home to North America's largest Mexican free-tailed bat population.

Journal:

Date(s) Visited:

Weather conditions:

Who you were with:

Nature observations:

Special memories:

Inner Space Cavern

Inner Space Cavern is one of the best-preserved caves in Texas. It was discovered in 1963 by the Texas Highway Department, but it's estimated to be about 20–25 million years old. The cave runs more than 65 feet deep.

It's also one of the only caves in which preserved animal fossils from the prehistoric Ice Age were excavated.

The cavern is located in Georgetown, Texas, just north of Austin. It's a perfect location for summer fun. The Inner Space Caverns see thousands of visitors a year. There are many activities to do nearby. For more adventurous folks, you can even take the hidden passage tours. Whatever tour you take, the caves have magnificent views and discoveries for everyone.

Best time to visit:
Winter, spring, or fall

Pass/Permit/Fees:
Ticket fees depend on tours, groups, and age.

Closest city or town:
Georgetown

How to get there:
From the north:
Exit 259 on I35 S toward Texas 26 Spur/Southeast Inner Loop
From the south:
Exit 259 B on I35 N toward SE Inner Loop Dr

GPS coordinates:
30.6079° N, 97.6881° W

Did you know?
The cavern was discovered after drilling through 40 feet of solid limestone.

Journal:

Date(s) Visited:

Weather
conditions:

Who you were with:

Nature observations:

Special memories:

Hamilton Pool Preserve

Hamilton Pool Preserve is one of the most beautiful swimming holes in all of Texas. Its clear blue water and high grotto is a summertime attraction for both Texans and out-of-state visitors.

Thousands of years ago, the ceiling to an underground river caved in, resulting in intense erosion. After several thousand more years, the erosion eventually formed the beautiful natural pool we know today as Hamilton Pool Preserve.

Take a short hike down to the grotto and you'll see a majestic waterfall. There is a small shoreline beach for tanning and playing when you're not swimming. The preserve itself has miles of trails to hike that will lead you out to the Pedernales River.

Best time to visit:
Summer

Pass/Permit/Fees:
Reservations are required for peak seasons. There is a fee for entry.

Closest city or town:
Austin

How to get there:
From the east: Drive west on US71 towards Hamilton Pool Road
From the west: Drive east on US71 towards Hamilton Pool Road

GPS coordinates:
30.3424° N, 98.1269° W

Did you know?
The preserve is home to the golden-cheeked warbler, a rare bird native to Texas.

Journal:

Date(s) Visited:

Weather
conditions:

Who you were with:

Nature observations:

Special memories:

Bluebonnet Fields

Bluebonnet fields are scattered all throughout the Lone Star State. As the state flower, bluebonnets blossom in the spring and can be seen in parks and yards, along highways, and anywhere else wildflowers grow.

This purple flower with a blue hue resembles the shape of a traditional woman's bonnet, hence its name. Although there isn't a specific field to go visit, there are plenty of fields that bloom in the springtime. Many Texans take their Easter photos in a field of bluebonnets. They only bloom for a few weeks each year, so it's important to visit when they're in full bloom.

Some of the best areas for bluebonnets, such as the Willow City Loop or Wildseed Farms, are along the Texas Hill Country region.

Best time to visit:
Late March through May

Pass/Permit/Fees:
None

Closest city or town:
N/A

How to get there:
N/A

GPS coordinates:
N/A

Did you know?
Texas Department of Transportation times its roadside mowing to allow for bluebonnets and other wildflowers to reseed for following years.

Journal:

Date(s) Visited:

Weather
conditions:

Who you were with:

Nature observations:

Special memories:

Guadalupe Mountains National Park

Guadalupe Mountains National Park is located in the large and vast Chihuahuan Desert of West Texas. It's home to the state's highest summit, Guadalupe Peak. From bloody battles between settlers and Apaches to the forming of a national park, Guadalupe Mountains National park offers over 10,000 years of human history.

In the mountains, you'll find drawings from early Apache tribes. While historians and archeologists have studied the drawings, none have been able to interpret their meanings. Guadalupe Mountains is a beautiful park filled with a rich history.

Best time to visit:
Year-round

Pass/Permit/Fees:
$10 per person

Closest city or town:
El Paso

How to get there:
Guadalupe Mountains National Park is located in far West Texas on U.S. Highway 62/180. The driving distance is 110 miles east of El Paso, Texas; 56 miles southwest of Carlsbad, New Mexico; or 62 miles north of Van Horn on Hwy 54.

GPS coordinates:
31.9231° N, 104.8645° W

Did you know?
The Guadalupe Mountains were once under water.

Journal:

Date(s) Visited:

Weather
conditions:

Who you were with:

Nature observations:

Special memories:

Jacob's Well

Jacob's Well is a sight to see. Its depth is both beautiful and a bit intimidating. While it's only 13 feet wide, the well is over 160 feet deep, making it extremely dangerous for deep-water diving. Dangling your feet from the edge of the well and looking down can feel like you're peering into the depths of the Earth through the clear blue water.

It's a summertime swimming favorite in the Texas Hill Country, though swimming is not permitted during certain times of year for water restoration purposes. There are many hiking trails for family and friends around the swimming hole as well. Dogs are not allowed.

Best time to visit:
If you'd like to swim, make reservations for after April 30th. Springtime is best for hiking and sightseeing, while summer is best for swimming in the well.

Pass/Permit/Fees:
Reservations required for swimming, but not visiting.

Closest city or town:
Wimberley

How to get there:
Jacob's Well Natural Area is located approximately 10 minutes from the city of Wimberley. The entrance to Jacob's Well Natural Area is located at 1699 Mt. Sharp Rd., Wimberley, TX 78676.

GPS coordinates:
30.0344° N, 98.1261° W

Did you know?
Jacob's Well is the second largest fully submerged cave in Texas.

Journal:

Date(s) Visited:

Weather conditions:

Who you were with:

Nature observations:

Special memories:

Enchanted Rock State Natural Area

As its name suggests, Enchanted Rock State Natural Area is a magnificent area of natural rock formation. This pink granite rock is close to the quaint town of Fredericksburg, Texas.

With its unparalleled beauty, the massive dome has attracted visitors for thousands of years. However, the dome isn't the only thing that's beautiful about Enchanted Rock. There are also many hiking trails, activities, and animal species to explore in the area.

Although swimming and biking are not allowed, you can try plenty of other activities like taking a long hike or stargazing in the open night sky. Enchanted Rock is a perfect nature-inspired getaway.

Best time to visit:
Spring is the best time to visit. Nature is in bloom and the Texas heat isn't as bad.

Pass/Permit/Fees:
Entrance fees depend on peak seasons and visitor age.

Closest city or town:
Fredericksburg

How to get there:
The park is 18 miles north of Fredericksburg on Ranch Road 965. From Llano, take State Highway 16 for 14 miles south and then go west on Ranch Road 965.

GPS coordinates:
30.5066° N, 98.8189° W

Did you know?
Humans have been camping in this area for over 12,000 years.

Journal:

Date(s) Visited:

Weather conditions:

Who you were with:

Nature observations:

Special memories:

The Natural Bridge Caverns

The Natural Bridge Caverns are the biggest caverns in the entire state of Texas, which makes this a top natural attraction. Geologists theorize that Texas was once under water, so the caverns are preserved with different layers of limestone, sedimentary rock, and fossils.

There are a number of different ways to see the caverns, from discovery tours to hidden passage tours. There are countless places to explore. Guided tours of the caves allow for more in-depth knowledge and learning about the caverns' rich prehistoric history from a professional.

Best time to visit:
Year-round

Pass/Permit/Fees:
Fees depend on tour selection and age of visitor.

Closest city or town:
San Antonio

How to get there:
Head north on I-35 and exit #175. Turn left (west) on Natural Bridge Caverns Road/F.M. 3009.

GPS coordinates:
29.6924° N, 98.3427° W

Did you know?
The caverns were formed from thousands of years of river water running through limestone.

Journal:

Date(s) Visited:

Weather conditions:

Who you were with:

Nature observations:

Special memories:

Lost Maples State Natural Area

Located just two hours northwest of San Antonio, Lost Maples State Natural Area is known for its fall foliage, but it boasts natural beauty all year round.

This natural area highlights that Texas does actually change with the four seasons. Lost Maples is home to bigtooth maple trees that are known for turning all shades of red, orange, and yellow during the autumn season.

There are miles of hiking trails, stargazing opportunities, and plenty of camping grounds for families and friends to enjoy throughout the year.

Best time to visit:
The fall is the most popular time, but there are activities open all year round.

Pass/Permit/Fees:
Fees depend on visitors' ages and group information.

Closest city or town:
Vanderpool

How to get there:

The park is located five miles north of Vanderpool on Ranch Road 187.

GPS coordinates:
29.8076° N, 99.5706° W

Did you know?
Lost Maples measures a 3 on the Bortle Dark-Sky Scale, which means there's enough darkness for viewing "celestial objects" like stars.

Journal:

Date(s) Visited:

Weather
conditions:

Who you were with:

Nature observations:

Special memories:

Caddo Lake State Park

Texas has a diverse landscape. From desert to tropics, it contains a wide range of wildlife, climates, and habitats. Caddo Lake Park is known for its piney landscape and features one of the only natural lakes in the state.

Caddo Lake is an East Texas state treasure. The cypress trees sprawl out of the water and create mossy canopies where you can canoe or fish.

You're welcome to camp, hike, look for a geocache, or boat in the park. There are historic cabins for rent for the less experienced camper, or 46 different campsites ranging from full hookups to water-only sites for the more rugged types.

Best time to visit:
Year-round

Pass/Permit/Fees:
Adult fees are $4. Children under 12 are free.

Closest city or town:
Karnack

How to get there:
Travel north of Karnack one mile on State Highway 43 to FM 2198. Go east for 0.5 miles to Park Road 2. The park is 15 miles northeast of Marshall.

GPS coordinates:
32.680233° N, 94.1790764° W

Did you know?
Caddo Indians were the original settlers of the land in the 18th or 19th centuries.

Journal:

Date(s) Visited:

Weather
conditions:

Who you were with:

Nature observations:

Special memories:

Davy Crockett National Forest

The Davy Crockett National Forest is named after the Texas hero and contains more than 160,000 acres of woodlands, streams, trails, recreation areas, camping grounds, and wildlife habitats in East Texas.

This national forest is located in both Houston and Trinity counties within the Neches and Trinity river basins. President Franklin Roosevelt made this land a national forest in 1936.

Since then, families, hikers, and adventurers have been visiting the forest for its miles of hiking trails within the East Texas landscape.

Best time to visit:
Spring is the perfect time to visit, though any mild temperatures and weather make for a great time in the forest.

Pass/Permit/Fees:
There are a number of different types of recreation passes available.

Closest city or town:
Crockett

How to get there:
From the west: head east on TX-7 through Kennard to Main Street
From the east: head west on TX-7 through Kennard to Main Street

GPS coordinates:
31.2970° N, 95.1020° W

Did you know?
Due to its location, there is a perfect blend of eastern and western birds that inhabit the forest, not seen anywhere else together in the state.

Journal:

Date(s) Visited:

Weather
conditions:

Who you were with:

Nature observations:

Special memories:

Padre Island National Seashore

Yes, Texas has beaches! South Padre Island is known as the site of some of Texas's most beautiful beaches. It features swimming, restaurants, and nightlife as well, so you can have an extended stay on the island. Located at the south tip of Texas, Padre Island National Seashore runs along the Gulf Coast and the Laguna Madre. Visiting this island is very much like stepping into the past because it is so well preserved. The shoreline does tend to get very crowded during the peak seasons and holidays, so be sure to plan your trip accordingly. There are a lot of outdoor activities, ranging from swimming to fishing and everything in between. There is something for everyone to enjoy.

Best time to visit:
For swimming, the best time to visit is summer. However, Padre Island National Seashore is open all year with plenty of activities.

Pass/Permit/Fees:
Fees vary based on age, vehicle, and season.

Closest city or town:
South Padre Island

How to get there:
To reach South Padre Island, get on Highway 77 and drive approximately three hours south of Corpus Christi.

GPS coordinates:
27.4738° N, 97.2852° W

Did you know?
Four countries have owned Padre Island at one point. In order, past owners include Spain, Mexico, Texas (when it was a country), and the United States.

Journal:

Date(s) Visited:

Weather conditions:

Who you were with:

Nature observations:

Special memories:

Rio Grande Valley

The Rio Grande Valley rises above the Rio Grande River, which separates the United States from Mexico. The valley is home to a diverse range of cultures and a beautiful blend of American and Mexican life.

The Rio Grande Valley, commonly known as simply "The Valley," is the southernmost point in Texas. The subtropical climate allows for warm to hot temperatures all year long.

In addition to its beaches and sunny weather, there are also wildlife preserves and areas for watching butterflies, reptiles, birds, and small mammals along the seashore.

Best time to visit:
The Rio Grande Valley features similar weather all year long with hot temperatures peaking in the summer.

Pass/Permit/Fees:
There are no passes or permits required to enjoy most of Rio Grande Valley, but there may be exceptions depending on which areas, parks, or reserves you visit.

Closest city or town:
Brownsville, TX

How to get there:
Head South on US-77 towards Brownsville and South Padre Island.

GPS coordinates:
26.2034° N, 98.2300° W

Did you know?
Each year, the Texas city of Brownsville and the Mexican city of Matamoros celebrate Charro Days, a three-day event celebrating a vibrant, lasting relationship between two international cities.

Journal:

Date(s) Visited:

Weather
conditions:

Who you were with:

Nature observations:

Special memories:

Monahans Sandhills State Park

Monahans Sandhills State Park is like Texas's biggest sandbox. The sand in this western part of the state forms into dunes and valleys and is a one-of-a-kind desert environment. Locals and Texans call this place *an ocean of sand*.

About a half hour's drive from Odessa, this state park contains over 3,800 acres and spans both Ward and Winkler counties.

Take time to explore the wildlife havens, hike on the sand dunes, or even walk through the mini forest. At the Monahans Sandhills State Park, there is an ever-changing landscape for you to enjoy.

Best time to visit:
Spring or fall. The cooler temperatures make visiting Monahans Sandhills State Park much more enjoyable.

Pass/Permit/Fees:
Adults 13 years and older have an entrance fee of $4. Children under 12 are free.

Closest city or town:
Odessa

How to get there:
To reach the park, travel along Interstate 20 and exit at mile marker 86 to Park Road 41.

GPS coordinates:
31.6189° N, 102.8120° W

Did you know?
There isn't any shade at Monahans Sandhills, so be careful with the sun's rays if you go during the day.

Journal:

Date(s) Visited:

Weather
conditions:

Who you were with:

Nature observations:

Special memories:

Seminole Canyon State Park

There's something truly magical about West Texas. It's the vision of Texas that folks around the United States imagine when they hear about the state. West Texas has tumbleweeds drifting on two-lane roads, desert mountains surrounded by blue skies, and places like Seminole Canyon State Park.

This park draws people in with its thousand-year-old pictographs from early Native Americans, but people stay for its beautiful scenery and the Rio Grande, which separates the United States and Mexico.

This southwest park is another treasure within Texas that's perfect for hiking and biking. It has 46 campsites, ranging from backwoods camping to full hookups with bathrooms on site.

Best time to visit:
Spring or fall. It can be dangerous outside in the summer, so if you go at that time, make sure to go in the early mornings before the hottest time of day.

Pass/Permit/Fees:
Adults 13 or older cost $4. Children under 12 are free.

Closest city or town:
Del Rio

How to get there:
The park is located nine miles west of Comstock on U.S. Highway 90, just east of the Pecos River Bridge.

GPS coordinates:
29.700094° N, 101.312875° W

Did you know?
There are pictographs that are over 7,000 years old at Seminole.

Journal:

Date(s) Visited:

Weather
conditions:

Who you were with:

Nature observations:

Special memories:

Marfa Lights

The Marfa Lights are said to be the most continuous supernatural occurrence to happen in Texas. People travel from around the world to see this mysterious phenomenon. It's still unproven exactly what these lights are. Some people say they are paranormal activity, while other, more cynical people will say they're atmospheric reflections of cars and campfires at night.

Whether you're a believer in the supernatural or not, the Marfa Lights are sure to elicit a puzzling reaction. What exactly *are* they? Sometimes, they're red, and other times, they're blue or white. They appear any time of year and in any type of weather.

If you'd like to see the lights for yourself, travel 9 miles west on Route US 90 and wait.

Best time to visit:
Any time of year. However, it's best to travel to Marfa in the spring, fall, or winter when it's not so hot.

Pass/Permit/Fees:
There are no passes or fees to see the Marfa Lights.

Closest city or town:
Marfa

How to get there:
The Marfa Lights Viewing Area is between Alpine and Marfa on US 90.

GPS coordinates:
30.3072° N, 104.0215° W

Did you know?
There have been reports of the Marfa Lights since the 19th century, and their cause is still unknown.

Journal:

Date(s) Visited:

Weather
conditions:

Who you were with:

Nature observations:

Special memories:

Davis Mountains State Park

There's no place more beautiful to stargaze at night than Davis Mountains State Park. Located high in the mountains in West Texas, this state park offers camping sites and miles of trails to hike.

Davis Mountains State Park is a great destination for those seeking a unique and remote experience. It's the right place for the more rugged adventurer. At Davis Mountains State Park, you can hike, backpack, mountain bike, go horseback riding, camp, stargaze, or study nature in all its glory. If camping isn't your thing, there is a lodge inside the park with full amenities as well.

Best time to visit:
Spring or fall. If visiting in the summer, be cautious of the heat and UV rays.

Pass/Permit/Fees:
Adults 13 years or older are $6. Children under 12 are free.

Closest city or town:
Fort Davis

How to get there:
Davis Mountain State Park is located one mile north of Fort Davis by taking Highway 17 to Highway 118N. The park's road is the third entrance, about three miles down 118N.

GPS coordinates:
30.5991° N, 103.9294° W

Did you know?
This park was one of the first projects of the Texas Civilian Conservation Corps, a project started by FDR during the Great Depression.

Journal:

Date(s) Visited:

Weather
conditions:

Who you were with:

Nature observations:

Special memories:

Devils River State Natural Area

In a remote location in West Texas lies pristine, nearly untouched waters and virtually endless miles of hiking and biking trails. Devils River State Natural Area is a majestic place, but it does take some work to get there.

Devils River State Natural Area offers visitors a quiet, off-the-beaten-path place for catch-and-release fishing, hiking, biking, and primitive camping. This natural area tends to experience flash flooding, so it's best to travel during the dryer seasons.

Best time to visit:
Spring or fall. Be sure to check weather conditions to avoid any flash flooding areas.

Pass/Permit/Fees:
Adults 13 years or older are $5. Children under 12 are free.

Closest city or town:
Del Rio

How to get there:
From Del Rio, go north on State Highway 277 for 45 miles, turn left on Dolan Creek Road (gravel) and go 18.6 miles to the SNA boundary. Dolan Creek Road is a rough, 22-mile gravel/dirt county road with multiple low-water crossings. Use caution if you see flowing water! This is working ranch country, so please drive carefully and be mindful of loose livestock.

GPS coordinates:
29.939694° N, 100.970206° W

Did you know?
Devils River State Natural Area has three ecosystems, making it a biologically diverse area.

Journal:

Date(s) Visited:

Weather
conditions:

Who you were with:

Nature observations:

Special memories:

Medina River

The Medina River lies on the south side of San Antonio. A quaint river that flows through a natural area, it has been attracting visitors and campers since its inception.

The Medina River Natural Area is a 511-acre property with seven miles of trails to hike and leisurely walk. During the spring, its banks are covered in beautiful Texas wildflowers. The area has a remarkable blend of pecan and cypress trees with blooming cactus, making it a quintessential stop for folks visiting the San Antonio area.

There are camping options as well. This natural area has a covered pavilion for small gatherings and camping amenities that can be rented by the hour.

Best time to visit:
Year-round. However, it's always best to avoid the hot Texas heat in the summer months.

Pass/Permit/Fees:
The only fees are for camping and renting the pavilion. These can vary.

Closest city or town:
San Antonio

How to get there:
From I-35, take exit 149 toward TX-422 Spur/TX-16/Poteet/Palo Alto Road. The Medina River Natural Area is located at 15890 Highway 16 South.

GPS coordinates:
29.263801° N, 98.578637° W

Did you know?
The Medina River is home to the green kingfisher and painted bunting.

Journal:

Date(s) Visited:

Weather conditions:

Who you were with:

Nature observations:

Special memories:

Pedernales State Park

A state park filled with limestone, rivers, and relaxation lies just thirty miles west of Austin. Pedernales State Park is located in Johnson City and offers visitors camping, hiking, and other outdoor adventures.

Swimming in the Pedernales River during the hot summer months can be a refreshing and relaxing break from everyday life. There is adventure around the park with its miles of hiking and mountain biking trails. You can even plan a stop at a nearby Texas gem, the Hamilton Pool Preserve.

Best time to visit:
Summer is the best time to visit for swimming if the river has enough water. Otherwise, it's beautiful all year round.

Pass/Permit/Fees:
Adults 13 years and older have a $6 entrance fee. Children under 12 are free.

Closest city or town:
Johnson City

How to get there:
The park may be reached by traveling 9 miles east of Johnson City on FM 2766, or by traveling west of Austin for 32 miles on U.S. Highway 290, then north on FM 3232 for 6 miles.

GPS coordinates:
30.3081° N, 98.2577° W

Did you know?
The park was privately owned until the state of Texas bought it in 1970.

Journal:

Date(s) Visited:

Weather conditions:

Who you were with:

Nature observations:

Special memories:

Krause Springs

The small town of Spicewood is home to a beautiful, quiet, and refreshing summer escape. This well-known, locally owned area is located in the beautiful Texas Hill Country. It offers guests a variety of summertime swimming options in a fresh, spring-fed pool or natural swimming hole.

Enjoy camping, swimming, picnicking, and other outdoor activities at Krause Springs. At the top of the property is a man-made pool that, due to the springs, is always at a cool, refreshing temperature.

Hike down just a bit and you'll find a natural swimming hole with a limestone beach to sunbathe and relax. Krause Springs is also known for its high rope swing; only the most adventurous dare to swing and plunge into the cold depths of the springs.

Best time to visit:
For swimming, the best time to visit is summer. If you'd like to hike or camp, spring is also a beautiful time to visit.

Pass/Permit/Fees:
Fees vary based on day, age, group, and camping selections.

Closest city or town:
Spicewood

How to get there:
From Austin, take Texas Highway 71 west. Cross the Pedernales River and drive 7 more miles. Turn right on Spur 191, then right again on County Road 404. The gates for Krause Springs are on the left.

GPS coordinates:
30.4777° N, 98.1517° W

Did you know?
There are a total of 32 natural springs on the property.

Journal:

Date(s) Visited:

Weather conditions:

Who you were with:

Nature observations:

Special memories:

Willow City Loop

Willow City Loop is the most vibrant, scenic drive in all of Texas Hill Country. While it's a magnificent sight year-round, making the trip during wildflower season is sure to be the show-stopping beauty you're looking for.

Willow City Loop is located near Fredericksburg, a small, romantic town in the Texas Hill Country known for its peaches, wineries, and local shopping. If you're visiting Fredericksburg, planning a scenic drive through Willow City Loop is a must.

The small, two-lane ranch road twists and turns for 13 miles through some of the oldest sites and habitats in Central Texas.

Best time to visit:
Spring, particularly wildflower season, which extends from late March toearly May. It's also recommended to go on a weekday, as weekends can be quite busy.

Pass/Permit/Fees:
There are no permits or fees.

Closest city or town:
Fredericksburg

How to get there:
Take 16N (Llano Street) out of Fredericksburg. Proceed 13.3 miles, then turn right on RR1323. Continue 2.79 miles to Willow City. Turn left onto Willow City Loop.

GPS coordinates:
30.4005° N, 98.7008° W

Did you know?
There are over ten types of wildflowers that bloom along the Willow City Loop.

Journal:

Date(s) Visited:

Weather
conditions:

Who you were with:

Nature observations:

Special memories:

Wildseed Farms

Wildseed Farms in Fredericksburg facilitates the beautification and preservation of Texas through its springtime wildflowers. The farm's founder, John R. Thomas, knew the importance of wildflowers and the joy they bring to the public. He turned a small seeding business into a wildflower farm for folks to visit and to ensure flowers blossom and grow by Texas highways.

Along with breathtaking views of dozens of species of wildflowers, visitors to Wildseed Farms can also enjoy cold beverages and other refreshments. If you're traveling and want to bring a piece of the Texas Hill Country back with you, they also have a plant nursery and sell wildflower seeds.

Best time to visit:
Wildflower season, which typically runs between March and October.

Pass/Permit/Fees:
This farm is open and free to the public.

Closest city or town:
Fredericksburg

How to get there:
Take HWY 290 in Fredericksburg to W/E Main St. The address is 100 Legacy Drive, Fredericksburg, TX 78624.

GPS coordinates:
30.2223° N, 98.7679° W

Did you know?
The farm has over 200 acres of wildflower fields.

Journal:

Date(s) Visited:

Weather conditions:

Who you were with:

Nature observations:

Special memories:

Boca Chica Beach

Boca Chica Beach is down in the southernmost point of the state in Brownsville. Recently, the beach has become notorious as the home of SpaceX, so traveling there can be tricky if not planned properly. Accessing the beach needs to be coordinated for times when it is open to the public.

Other than being home to SpaceX, Boca Chica Beach sits along the Gulf Shore and is known as America's "Third Coast." This beach is a semblance of where the United States ends, and Mexico begins. Once a rapid river spilling into the Gulf, it's now a quaint and nearly untouched stretch of beach and nature.

Best time to visit:
It's best to check when the beach is open to the public due to SpaceX activities.

Pass/Permit/Fees:
There are no fees.

Closest city or town:
Brownsville

How to get there:
Take I-69E towards TX-4 until you arrive at Boca Chica State Park.

GPS coordinates:
25.9965° N, 97.1501° W

Did you know?
Although Texas beaches have many visitors each year, Boca Chica Beach only gets a few, making it a relaxing beach compared to neighboring ones.

Journal:

Date(s) Visited:

Weather
conditions:

Who you were with:

Nature observations:

Special memories:

Granbury City Beach Park

Granbury City Beach Park is a cozy stop southwest of Fort Worth. This small beach offers boardwalks, picnic tables, and sandy shores along Lake Granbury.

The City of Granbury is a historic town, and this park is one of its main attractions. Offering pleasant strolls along its boardwalk, swimming, a pavilion for outdoor activities, and kayaking, it's a must for families looking for a summer getaway in the northern part of the state.

While the park does not offer overnight camping, it is a perfect day trip destination. The City of Granbury has a variety of hotels and bed-and-breakfasts for you to choose from if you'd like an extended stay in the area.

Best time to visit:
Granbury City Beach Park is a great place to visit in the summer for its swimming and beach activities.

Pass/Permit/Fees:
There are no passes or fees required.

Closest city or town:
Granbury

How to get there:
Take US-377 S to E Pearl St in Granbury.

GPS coordinates:
32.4418° N, 97.7813° W

Did you know?
Lake Granbury is a man-made reservoir that was constructed in 1969.

Journal:

Date(s) Visited:

Weather
conditions:

Who you were with:

Nature observations:

Special memories:

Island View Park

Island View Park is about an hour and a half north of Dallas/Fort Worth in Pottsboro. A sandy beach and summer attraction for North Texans, it's a refreshing day trip getaway for out of towners as well.

The beach offers sandy shores along Lake Texoma. Guests can enjoy summertime activities like swimming, kayaking, paddleboarding, picnic areas, sunset evening boat rides, and a number of beach sports.

Pets are also welcome at Island View Park as long as they're on a leash. Shelters for gatherings and events can also be rented by the hour or day.

Best time to visit:
For swimming and other water activities, summer is the best time. If you'd just like to enjoy the view or have a picnic, spring is also a great option!

Pass/Permit/Fees:
$7 entrance fee per person. Kids under 7 are free.

Closest city or town:
Pottsboro

How to get there:
From the south: Take I35 N towards US75 N. Take Exit 70.
From the north: Take I35 S towards US75 S. Take Exit 70.

GPS coordinates:
33.8595463°N, -96.6711079°W

Did you know?
Lake Texoma is one of the largest reservoirs in the country. It separates Texas from Oklahoma.

Journal:

Date(s) Visited:

Weather
conditions:

Who you were with:

Nature observations:

Special memories:

Jamaica Beach

Jamaica Beach is located in Galveston County along Texas's Gulf Shore. It's a small beach city with welcoming shore vibes that make it a quaint summer getaway.

If you're not a fan of popular tourist spots, Jamaica Beach is the city for you. Unlike bigger attractions along the Gulf Shore, like South Padre Island and Port Aransas, Jamaica Beach attracts a much calmer crowd.

According to the 2010 census, the population of Jamaica Beach is only 983 people. So, if you plan on an extended stay in the area, you may just become a local yourself!

Best time to visit:
Spring or summer for warm-weather activities like swimming, kayaking, and camping.

Pass/Permit/Fees:
Jamaica Beach doesn't require a pass to visit the town, but there may be fees for entrance to certain attractions and beaches in the city.

Closest city or town:
Jamaica Beach

How to get there:
Follow I-10 E to TX-342 Sput S/Broadway St in Galveston. Take exit 1A from 1-45 S.

GPS coordinates:
29.1897° N, 94.9796° W

Did you know?
Before becoming a town, Jamaica Beach was a burial ground for the Karankawa people.

Journal:

Date(s) Visited:

Weather conditions:

Who you were with:

Nature observations:

Special memories:

Little Elm Beach

Little Elm Park is located along Lake Lewisville, northwest of Plano. It contains a beautiful, refreshing, and energizing beach. Equipped with a handful of beach volleyball nets, Little Elm Beach offers some of the largest open swimming locations for Texans and out-of-state visitors to enjoy during the hot summer months.

Along with its impressive volleyball courts, the beach offers paddle-boarding, kayaking, swimming, and bike rentals from a nearby surf shop.

The park also has beachside dining at their Lakefront Grill, or you can always bring your own food and have a picnic with family and friends. The surrounding area has food and drink options for you to enjoy, and the summer offers lots of things to do for all ages.

Best time to visit:
For swimming and water activities, summer is the best month to visit Little Elm Beach.

Pass/Permit/Fees:
There is no fee for entrance, but you may have to pay for events and other activities along the beach.

Closest city or town:
Little Elm

How to get there:
Follow I35 N to S Interstate 35 S. Take exit 458.

GPS coordinates:
33.1587° N, 96.9484° W

Did you know?
Little Elm Beach is located inside Little Elm Park.

Journal:

Date(s) Visited:

Weather conditions:

Who you were with:

Nature observations:

Special memories:

Magnolia Beach

Magnolia Beach sits along the Texas coastline. Unlike many beaches, this one offers hard sand, making it easy for cars, trucks, and RVs to drive and camp on the shoreline.

The beach stretches 1.5 miles along Matagorda Bay, which is about 20 minutes south of the small town of Port Lavaca. While this isn't your typical vacation beach, it does offer a peaceful getaway for avid campers and RVers to escape. There are beautiful views of water and sand.

However, quiet and picturesque comes at a cost. There aren't a lot of amenities in the surrounding town, so it's recommended to bring all of your essentials before parking on Magnolia Beach.

Best time to visit:
Spring or summer. Summer if you'd like to go swimming!

Pass/Permit/Fees:
There are no permits or fees to park your car at Magnolia Beach.

Closest city or town:
Port Lavaca

How to get there:
Take TX-130 S, US-183 S, and US-87 S to FM 2433 in Calhoun County. Take exit 223 toward TX-45Toll/FM 1327/Creedmoor.

GPS coordinates:
28.5603° N, 96.5428° W

Did you know?
Because the Colorado and Lavaca rivers flow through this beach, it is less salty than the Gulf of Mexico.

Journal:

Date(s) Visited:

Weather conditions:

Who you were with:

Nature observations:

Special memories:

Matagorda Bay Nature Park

Along Texas's Gulf Coast, there is a majestic and natural area filled with beauty, adventure, and refreshing water to escape the oppressive Texas heat. The Matagorda Bay Nature area spans 1,300 acres of marshes, beaches, and wetland areas.

Matagorda Nature Park also has options for every type of camper. From the glamper to the rugged, backwoods type, there are options for everyone. The park has two airstream trailers that can be rented out with full amenities like air conditioning and running water. There is also an RV park and campsites for you to enjoy. At Matagorda Nature Park, you can enjoy a number of water activities, including swimming, boating, and fishing as well as land activities like birdwatching, horseback riding, and mini golf.

Best time to visit:
Summer, but the park offers activities all year round.

Pass/Permit/Fees:
There are varying fees for entry based on age, lodging, and other factors.

Closest city or town:
Matagorda

How to get there:
Follow TX-71 to FM 1468 Hwy N in Matagorda County. Turn right onto TX-35 S. Continue on FM1468 to Wadsworth. Turn right onto TX-60 S, then left onto FM2031.

GPS coordinates:
28.5505° N, 96.3013° W

Did you know?
Matagorda Bay Nature Park is part of the Lower Colorado River Authority (LCRA).

Journal:

Date(s) Visited:

Weather
conditions:

Who you were with:

Nature observations:

Special memories:

Mustang Island

Mustang Island, home of Selena Quintanilla, is a small coastal town known for its Mexican culture. It also offers a beautiful state park beach with sandy stretches for sunbathing, cool water for swimming, and plenty of campsites for visitors to enjoy on summer vacation.

Mustang Island State Park sits on the edge of Corpus Christi, just south of Port Aransas. The beach offers over five miles of shoreline and activities like fishing, swimming, surfing, and camping. If you're looking for a park to escape to in the summer, Mustang Island is a Texas must see!

Best time to visit:
Summer

Pass/Permit/Fees:
Adults above the age of 13 are $5. Children under the age of 12 are free.

Closest city or town:
Corpus Christi

How to get there:
To reach the park, travel southeast from Corpus Christi on State Highway 358 to Padre Island, then cross the JFK Causeway. Continue one mile to the traffic light and turn left onto State Highway 361 (formerly Park Road 53). Go five miles north to park headquarters for a total distance of about 22 miles. The physical address of the park is 17047 State Highway 361.

GPS coordinates:
27.7104° N, 97.1629° W

Did you know?
Mustang Island was named after the wild horses that once roamed the beach.

Journal:

Date(s) Visited:

Weather conditions:

Who you were with:

Nature observations:

Special memories:

North Beach

North Beach is another Corpus Christi must-see stop along the Texas shoreline. This sunny Gulf Coast beach is home to some of Corpus Christi's most famous attractions, like the Texas State Aquarium and the *USS Lexington*, a museum that was once an active aircraft carrier.

North Beach offers visitors tons of activities and amenities, including fishing, playgrounds, dining, museums, and more. There's really something for everyone in the family. North Beach also has a handful of beachfront hotels and resorts to enjoy extended stays along the coast.

Best time to visit:
Summer is a great time to visit for swimming and water activities, but there are attractions and things to do all year long at North Beach.

Pass/Permit/Fees:
There are no permits or fees to enter North Beach, but there are fees for various attractions.

Closest city or town:
Corpus Christi

How to get there:
Follow I-35 S and I-37 S to Seagull Blvd in Corpus Christi. Take the exit toward Texas State Aquarium/USS Lexington/North Beach from TX-35 N/US-181 N. Drive to Surfside Blvd.

GPS coordinates:
27.8211° N, 97.3903° W

Did you know?
North Beach consists of 1.5 miles of coastline along the Gulf of Mexico.

Journal:

Date(s) Visited:

Weather conditions:

Who you were with:

Nature observations:

Special memories:

Port Aransas Beach

Known to locals and Texans alike as "Port A," Port Aransas is one of Texas's top summer destinations along the Gulf Coast. Home to popular attractions like Beachtoberfest, Art Fiesta Weekend, and the Harvest Moon Regatta, this beachy town is a hotspot for those wanting to enjoy some summertime fun in Texas.

Port Aransas consists of 5 miles of coastline along the 18-mile barrier island. Barrier Islands like Port A protect the islands from destructive hurricanes, waves, and other natural disasters.

If you're looking for a Texas hotspot to escape to for a summer vacation of family fun, Port Aransas is sure to have activities for everyone to enjoy.

Best time to visit:
Port A is a popular Texas summer destination.

Pass/Permit/Fees:
There are no fees to enter Port Aransas, but there may be fees for certain activities along its beaches.

Closest city or town:
Port Aransas

How to get there:
Take I-37 S to S Padre Island Dr/Park Rd 22 in Corpus Christi, then
take TX-361 N to Port Aransas Beach Rd in Port Aransas.

GPS coordinates:
27.8274° N, 97.0530° W

Did you know?
The island of Port Aransas was first known as "Wild Horse Island" because of the wild horses the Spaniards brought to the area in the 1800s.

Journal:

Date(s) Visited:

Weather conditions:

Who you were with:

Nature observations:

Special memories:

Rockport Beach

Rockport Beach in Aransas County is located on the Gulf Coast. It stretches along Aransas Bay and is a popular tourist attraction for summer vacationers to the Texas shoreline.

If traveling to Rockport, stop at Rockport Beach Park for some daytime fun. The park features a saltwater pool, boat ramps, pavilions for small or larger gatherings, and plenty of swimming for all ages.

The beach is home to whooping cranes, which fly down to Aransas County in the wintertime. It's also a popular spot for birdwatching, fishing, and other outdoor summer activities.

Best time to visit:
For swimming and water activities, it's best to visit in the summer. However, the beach is open to visitors year-round.

Pass/Permit/Fees:
Parking fees are required.

Closest city or town:
Rockport

How to get there:
Take US-77 S to TX239 Ramp to Tivoli/Goliad, then turn left on TX-239 E. Keep right to continue on TX-35 S.

GPS coordinates:
28.0272° N, 97.0456° W

Did you know?
Live oaks fill the town of Rockport. It's home to the state's famous live oak, named "The Big Tree."

Journal:

Date(s) Visited:

Weather
conditions:

Who you were with:

Nature observations:

Special memories:

Seawall Urban Park

Seawall Urban Park, located near Galveston Beach, marries the beauty of nature and the accessibility of urban living. Known for its summertime fun, it's a refreshing place to escape the oppressive Texas heat.

Seawall Urban Park offers visitors tons of activities. The urban park stretches along for 10 miles and is home to the nation's longest and continuous sidewalk. This makes it a perfect place for running, biking, or taking a leisurely stroll with family and friends.

In addition to the summertime amenities along its coastline, Seawall Urban Park also has many beachfront restaurants, resorts, and attractions for tourists to the area.

Best time to visit:
The most common time for visitors to tour Seawall Urban Park is the summer, but the park is open to the public year-round.

Pass/Permit/Fees:
There are parking fees required to enter. You may not park or drive on the beach.

Closest city or town:
Galveston

How to get there:
Follow I-10 E and I-45 S to Broadway Avenue J in Galveston, then continue on Broadway Avenue J to Seawall Blvd.

GPS coordinates:
29.3015° N, 94.7739° W

Did you know?
Seawall Urban Park is along Seawall Boulevard, which is central to Galveston's tourist attractions.

Journal:

Date(s) Visited:

Weather
conditions:

Who you were with:

Nature observations:

Special memories:

South Padre Beach

All the way at the tip of the state, where Texas ends and Mexico begins, there's a place filled with wildlife, summer fun, and lots of opportunities. South Padre Beach is one of Texas's most beautiful and popular beach destinations. This barrier island separates Texas from the Gulf of Mexico, sitting between it and Laguna Madre. When traveling to South Padre, you're surrounded by water and palm trees.

There is so much to do on this island. If nature and adventure are more your style, there are wildlife preserves and centers for you to explore. But if you're more into the nightlife, then there are a number of beachfront restaurants and resorts for you to enjoy as well.

Best time to visit:
Hands-down, the best time to visit South Padre is the summer. However, it does get very crowded during popular summer holidays.

Pass/Permit/Fees:
Depending on the activity, there may be fees to enter. Entering the town itself is free of charge.

Closest city or town:
Brownsville

How to get there:
Take US-77 S to Cameron County. Exit onto TX-550, then merge onto TX-48 E. Turn right onto State Park Rd 100. Continue onto TX-100 E/Queen Isabella Causeway. Turn left onto Padre Blvd.

GPS coordinates:
26.1118° N, 97.1681° W

Did you know?
You can take snorkeling tours, dolphin watch, or visit sea turtle rescue centers.

Journal:

Date(s) Visited:

Weather
conditions:

Who you were with:

Nature observations:

Special memories:

Surfside Beach

Known to locals simply as "Surfside," this Texas beach town offers visitors a charming, quiet place to escape to in the summer. This beach is located on Follet's Island along the Gulf of Mexico.

This tiny beach town is a perfect contrast to popular beaches like Port A or South Padre. If you're looking for a more low-key, relaxing vibe, this is your dream destination. In 2010, the US Census recorded the population of this small town as just 482 people.

Best time to visit:
For water activities, it's best to visit Surfside in the summer, but the town is beautiful and quaint all year round.

Pass/Permit/Fees:
There are no fees to enter Surfside Beach.

Closest city or town:
Surfside Beach

How to get there:
Take I-10 to Exit 699 toward FM102/Eagle Lake. Follow FM102 S to E Main St. in Eagle Lake. Follow US-90 ALT E to Beasley Rd/Farm-To-Market Rd 1875/FM 1875 Rd in Fort Bend County. Continue on Farm-To-Market Rd 1875, then take FM 360 Rd to TX-36 S in Needville.
Follow TX-36 S, TX-35 N, and State Hwy 288 S to TX-332 E in Lake Jackson. Take the TX-332 E exit from State Hwy 288 S.

GPS coordinates:
33.6060° N, 78.9731° W

Did you know?
Former congressman Ron Paul owns a beach home in Surfside.

Journal:

Date(s) Visited:

Weather conditions:

Who you were with:

Nature observations:

Special memories:

Westcave Waterfalls

Westcave Waterfalls is about 45 minutes west of Austin. It's located near Hamilton Pool, which is equally beautiful. So, if you're traveling in this area, you must stop and see both.

Westcave Waterfalls is located in the Westcave Discovery Center, which prioritizes the preservation and protection of our natural habitats and resources.

This center is all about conservation, collaboration, and educating its visitors to be more sustainable and environmentally friendly citizens. Stopping by Westcave Waterfalls will be both an educational and inspiring adventure.

Best time to visit:
Spring or summer, as this is when the area is lush with greenery and many native plants are in bloom.

Pass/Permit/Fees:
$60 per household group.

Closest city or town:
Road Mountain

How to get there:
Take Hwy 290 to Fitzhugh Rd. Turn left on Hamilton Pool Rd.

GPS coordinates:
30.339045° N, 98.140838° W

Did you know?
You'll find a lot of native plants on this preserve, including the Texas persimmon, Ashe juniper, Texas live oak, and dozens more.

Journal:

Date(s) Visited:

Weather conditions:

Who you were with:

Nature observations:

Special memories:

Capote Falls

Right outside of Marfa, way out in West Texas, Capote Falls is the state's biggest and proudest waterfall. It stands at an amazing 175 ft tall; everything is bigger here, after all. For a state that's known for its deserts, Texas has some beautiful waterfalls as well, and Capote Falls makes it to the top of the list.

Unfortunately, this waterfall is privately owned and can only be seen by air, unless you know the owners, of course. Because of its lack of visitors, it's in pristine condition, and the surrounding habitat is preserved.

You may not be able to swim in Capote Falls but seeing its beauty from the air is a rare gift only a few get to enjoy.

Best time to visit:
The best time to visit is unknown as it doesn't accept public guests.

Pass/Permit/Fees:
There are no passes, permits, or fees.

Closest city or town:
Marfa

How to get there:
N/A

GPS coordinates:
30.2143° N, 104.5596° W

Did you know?
The waterfall drains into the Rio Grande Rift and the Sierra Vieja, which flow towards the Rio Grande River.

Date(s) visited:

Journal:

Date(s) Visited:

Weather conditions:

Who you were with:

Nature observations:

Special memories:

Gorman Falls

Gorman Falls is two hours northwest of Austin. It's a beautiful state park that many Austinites and other locals love to visit. Gorman State Park is also home to Gorman Falls and Spicewood Springs.

This state park is a relaxing destination for those who want to cool off, fish, paddle, or boat along its waters. It also offers over 35 miles of hiking and bike trails for folks to explore. You can even go on a self-guided tour of the waterfalls, which is a 3-mile roundtrip hike.

The park offers guests a more rugged camping experience, with sites that are meant for backwoods campers. There are some campsites that have water, but no hookups.

Best time to visit:
Spring or fall, when the weather isn't too hot.

Pass/Permit/Fees:
Adults 13 years and older are $5. Children under 12 are free.

Closest city or town:
Lometa

How to get there:
Take I-35, US-183 N, Route 183A N, and US-183 N to W. North Ave in Lampasas. Take Farm to Market Rd. 580 to Gorman Rd. in San Saba County.

GPS coordinates:
31.022965° N, 98.442401° W

Did you know?
Texas Parks and Wildlife purchased this park in 1984.

Journal:

Date(s) Visited:

Weather
conditions:

Who you were with:

Nature observations:

Special memories:

Cattails Falls

Surprisingly, there is a moderately known hiking spot near Big Bend National Park that ends in a cascading oasis. What makes its relative secrecy so special is the beautiful paradise at the end of the hike: Cattails Falls.

The hike is only about 1.5 miles into the canyon. It's not recommended to take these hikes in the summer, as the heat can be aggressive and dangerous for even the most experienced hikers. Sometimes, drought years offer a less-than-exciting end. So, be sure that you hike here when the region has seen a decent amount of rainfall.

Once you escape the desert and enter into more of the lush greenery, be on the lookout for wild black bears!

Best time to visit:
Spring or summer

Pass/Permit/Fees:
Cattails Falls is located in Big Bend National Park, so it is subject to their passes and fees.

Closest city or town:
Terlingua

How to get there:
Head south on Ross Maxwell Scenic Drive in Big Bend. After mile marker 3, look for a small opening beyond the Sam Nail Ranch overlook. It's easy to miss, so be on the lookout!

GPS coordinates:
29.2731° N, 103.3355° W

Did you know?
Only the most seasoned Big Bend hikers travel to Cattails Falls every year.

Journal:

Date(s) Visited:

Weather conditions:

Who you were with:

Nature observations:

Special memories:

Dolan Falls

Dolan Falls Preserves is fed by two popular and beautiful springs where West Texas meets the Hill Country. Devils River and Dolan Creek feed into this preserve, and locals boast that it is one of Texas's most pristine destinations to visit.

This nature preserve consists of 4,788 acres. In it, you'll experience the intersection of three distinct climates from the Edwards Plateau, Chihuahuan Desert, and the Rio Grande Plain. The combination of these terrains and habitats results in magnificent, unparalleled beauty.

Unfortunately, Dolan Falls is not open to the public. However, neighboring Devils River State Natural Area is open year-round.

Best time to visit:
The best time to visit is unknown as it doesn't accept public guests.

Pass/Permit/Fees:
There are no passes, permits, or fees.

Closest city or town:
Del Rio

How to get there:
N/A

GPS coordinates:
29.8844° N, 100.9934° W

Did you know?
The Nature Conservancy owns this land, and its main priority is to keep it preserved and protected. That's why public visitors are not allowed.

Journal:

Date(s) Visited:

Weather
conditions:

Who you were with:

Nature observations:

Special memories:

Boykin Springs

There's another gem in East Texas that folks ought to see. Boykin Springs Recreation Area sits on Boykin Springs Lake within Angelina National Forest. This spot offers something for everyone. At Boykin Springs, you can camp, hike, bike, fish, picnic, or just relax in nature.

The recreation area also has a pavilion and picnic area that can accommodate a reservation up to 74 people for a larger gathering.

Although there are no water hookups for campers, there are hot showers and running water for you to enjoy. Boykin Springs is a great trip for the rugged camper or day-tripper.

Best time to visit:
Spring or fall

Pass/Permit/Fees:
The park is free to enter, but there are fees for camping and renting the picnic area.

Closest city or town:
Zavalla

How to get there:
From Zavalla, travel east on Highway 63 for 10 miles. Turn right on Forest Service Road 313 and continue for 2 miles to the campground.

GPS coordinates:
31.06161940° N, 94.27461500° W

Did you know?
Archeologists predict that humans have inhabited this land for 8,000 years.

Journal:

Date(s) Visited:

Weather
conditions:

Who you were with:

Nature observations:

Special memories:

Waco Mammoth National Monument

Waco Mammoth National Monument sits along the Bosque River in North Texas and has over 100 acres of woodland.

It's known for the mammoth fossils found in the park in the 1970s. Thousands of years ago, during the Ice Age, this region was home to the massive Columbian mammoth.

This national monument is covered in Texas's very own oak, cedar, and mesquite trees. It also offers hiking and camping opportunities along with its rich history.

Best time to visit:
Spring or fall

Pass/Permit/Fees:
Fees vary based on age and occupation. There are discounts for military members, educators, students, and children.

Closest city or town:
Waco

How to get there:
From the north: Take exit 339 off I-35 North. Lake Shore Drive will be on your right. Take another right onto Steinbeck Bend Drive and continue for another 1.5 miles until you reach the monument.

From the south: Take exit 335C off I-35 S. Make a left at Martin Luther King, Jr. Blvd. Continue on Steinbeck Bend Drive, and you'll see the monument in 1.5 miles.

GPS coordinates:
31.6067° N, 97.1758° W

Did you know?
16 Columbian mammoth fossils were found here from 1978 to 1990.

Journal:

Date(s) Visited:

Weather
conditions:

Who you were with:

Nature observations:

Special memories:

Big Thicket National Preserve

Big Thicket National Preserve is about an hour and a half northeast of Houston and contains nine different ecosystems. There's something for everyone in this diverse, lush land.

This natural preserve protects and prioritizes the diverse wildlife, animals, and insects within its borders. There are miles of trails and waterways for folks to either hike or canoe along. From the tall cypress trees to the low bayous, the range of ecosystems will leave you inspired and excited to spend a camping trip in this national park.

Best time to visit:
Spring or fall

Pass/Permit/Fees:
There are no passes or fees to enter.

Closest city or town:
Kountze

How to get there:
There isn't a main entrance to the preserve, but there is a visitor center. The best route is to follow I-10 E to Wallisville. Take exit 812 from I-10 E and turn left onto TX-61 N. Then, turn right onto US-90 E and left onto TX-326 N/Old U.S. 90. Use the left two lanes to turn left onto US-287 N/US-69 N/S Pine St. Turn right onto FM 420 E.

GPS coordinates:
30.458251° N, 94.387285° W

Did you know?
The increase in infrastructure and industry is what eventually drove Big Thicket to become a national preserve in 1974.

Journal:

Date(s) Visited:

Weather
conditions:

Who you were with:

Nature observations:

Special memories:

Lake Conroe

Although it's named Lake Conroe, this lake is only partially in the city of Conroe. The rest of the lake is in Montgomery County.

This 22,000-acre lake offers two swimming areas, fishing piers, playgrounds, and picnic areas along its coastline. It's a relatively quiet place to travel to in Northeast Texas, but it's great for family camping activities and day trips.

In addition to the lake's amenities, you can also find activities and events like beach volleyball and horseshoe games for a friendly competition with your group.

Best time to visit:
The lake is open year-round, but the best time to visit for warm-weather activities is in late spring or summer, as they're only open seasonally.

Pass/Permit/Fees:
There are no permits, passes, or fees, but you may need to pay for activities like boating and fishing.

Closest city or town:
Conroe

How to get there:
Follow US-290 E to W. Blue Bell Rd in Brenham. Take TX-105 E to FM 1097 E in Montgomery County.

GPS coordinates:
30.4369° N, 95.5985° W

Did you know?
Lake Conroe was built as an alternate water source for Houston, Texas, in 1973.

Journal:

Date(s) Visited:

Weather conditions:

Who you were with:

Nature observations:

Special memories:

Lake Bob Sandlin State Park

In Texas's vastness, you're sure to find a variety of ecosystems, climates, and species of wildlife. Lake Bob Sandlin State Park is unique because it's where two of these ecosystems meet. While visiting this state park, you'll see giant trees to the east and the tall grasses of the Texas Plains to the west.

East Texas is known for its swampland and lush greenery. Lake Bob Sandlin State Park has acres of forest along the lake's shoreline, where guests can fish, boat, hike, bike, and nature watch.

Whoever thinks Texas doesn't show a change in the seasons is wrong. At Lake Bob Sandlin, autumn boasts beautiful fall foliage and is a must-see stop for anyone traveling in the area.

Best time to visit:
Fall is the best time to view the foliage.

Pass/Permit/Fees:
Adults 13 years or younger are $4. Children under 12 are free.

Closest city or town:
Pittsburgh

How to get there:
Lake Bob Sandlin State Park is approximately 12 miles southwest of Mount Pleasant. Take Interstate 30 to Highway 37 S at Mount Vernon and continue for 0.8 miles. Turn left onto Highway 21. The park entrance is 11.2 miles down.

GPS coordinates:
33.053955° N, 95.099155° W

Did you know?
The Caddo people called East Texas home from the year 800 through 1860, which included the land in Lake Bob Sandlin State Park.

Journal:

Date(s) Visited:

Weather
conditions:

Who you were with:

Nature observations:

Special memories:

Lake Fork

When we think of coasts and shores in Texas, we often think of the Gulf of Mexico. People often underestimate the natural beauty of the state's reservoirs and lakes. Down here, they say, "Life is better at the lake."

If you're searching for that, then travel 65 miles east of Dallas, where you'll find Lake Fork on Lake Fork Creek. Lake Fork is over 27,000 acres and offers over 300 miles of coastline! It's the perfect spot for vacationers to stop and enjoy fishing, boating, swimming, and other water activities, as well as hiking and biking along its scenic shores.

Best time to visit:
It's beautiful all year, but the best time to visit Lake Fork is in the spring, fall, or summer.

Pass/Permit/Fees:
It's free to visit Lake Fork, but depending on the activities you choose, you may need to pay a fee for entry.

Closest city or town:
Lake Fork

How to get there:
From Dallas: Get on I-20 E in Mesquite via E. Malloy Bridge Rd. Follow I-20 E, TX-34 N, and TX-276 E to FM 515 E/Lake Fork Dr. in Emory. Follow FM 515 E and Co Rd 1970 to Peninsula Dr. in Wood County.

GPS coordinates:
32.8311° N, 95.5830° W

Did you know?
Lake Fork is known for its largemouth bass fishing. In fact, it currently holds the records for the top 34 largemouth bass caught in the state of Texas.

Journal:

Date(s) Visited:

Weather
conditions:

Who you were with:

Nature observations:

Special memories:

Other Places

Place:

Date(s) visited:

Weather conditions:

Who you were with:

Nature observations:

Special memories:

Place: _____

Date(s) visited:

Weather conditions:

Who you were with:

Nature observations:

Special memories:

Place: _____

Date(s) visited:

Weather conditions:

Who you were with:

Nature observations:

Special memories:

108

Place: _____

Date(s) visited:

Weather conditions:

Who you were with:

Nature observations:

Special memories:

Place: _____

Date(s) visited:

Weather conditions:

Who you were with:

Nature observations:

Special memories:

Place: _____

Date(s) visited:

Weather conditions:

Who you were with:

Nature observations:

Special memories:

Place: _____

Date(s) visited:

Weather conditions:

Who you were with:

Nature observations:

Special memories:

Place: _____

Date(s) visited:

Weather conditions:

Who you were with:

Nature observations:

Special memories:

Place: _____

Date(s) visited:

Weather conditions:

Who you were with:

Nature observations:

Special memories:

Place: _____

Date(s) visited:

Weather conditions:

Who you were with:

Nature observations:

Special memories:

Credit the Incredible Photographers:

Texas State Map
https://www.shutterstock.com/image-vector/texas-map-icon-vector-illustration-763517677
Holovatiuk, D. (n.d.). Texas Map Icon. Vector Illustration. Shutterstock.
https://www.shutterstock.com/image-vector/texas-map-icon-vector-illustration-763517677.

Big Bend National Park
https://search.creativecommons.org/photos/f72880a1-83f2-4f43-b263-a7213051d3a5
"Tree and Bird, Big Bend National Park" by AlphaTangoBravo / Adam Baker is licensed with CC
BY 2.0. To view a copy of this license, visit https://creativecommons.org/licenses/by/2.0/

Palo Duro Canyon
https://search.creativecommons.org/photos/0a827014-5367-490a-80b6-a8bcaa3ab774
"Lighthouse - Palo Duro Canyon, Texas" by Thomas Shahan 3 is licensed with CC BY 2.0. To
view a copy of this license, visit https://creativecommons.org/licenses/by/2.0/

Lady Bird Lake
https://search.creativecommons.org/photos/ead390c3-f062-459c-8409-9d3d6acf6bad
"Lady Bird Lake from dock" by Tim Patterson is licensed with CC BY-SA 2.0. To view a copy of
this license, visit https://creativecommons.org/licenses/by-sa/2.0/

Inner Space Cavern
https://search.creativecommons.org/photos/c27d66d8-c018-4843-89a6-27068d82ae04
"The deepest gallery of Inner Space Caverns" by Lars Plougmann is licensed with CC BY-SA 2.0.
To view a copy of this license, visit https://creativecommons.org/licenses/by-sa/2.0/

Hamilton Pool Preserve
https://search.creativecommons.org/photos/19571d9d-966d-4be7-af9c-7aea2925dbdf
"Hamilton Pool Preserve" by danmcgrotty is licensed with CC BY 2.0. To view a copy of this
license, visit https://creativecommons.org/licenses/by/2.0/

Bluebonnet Field
https://search.creativecommons.org/photos/97e74342-7d6e-440e-8686-c1c743605664
"Texas Bluebonnets" by Jeff Pang is licensed with CC BY 2.0. To view a copy of this license, visit
https://creativecommons.org/licenses/by/2.0/

Guadalupe Mountains National Park
https://search.creativecommons.org/photos/14682aa5-d256-4763-b875-c22e610dedea
"Guadalupe Mountains National Park" by Thomas Shahan 3 is licensed with CC BY 2.0. To view
a copy of this license, visit https://creativecommons.org/licenses/by/2.0/

Jacob's Well
https://search.creativecommons.org/photos/51c61f1c-4c3e-403e-b2c1-38e38ea9199b
"File:Jacobs well.jpg" by Aleksomber is licensed with CC BY-SA 4.0. To view a copy of this
license, visit https://creativecommons.org/licenses/by-sa/4.0

Enchanted Rock State Natural Area
https://search.creativecommons.org/photos/8b1446cc-8941-47f9-a172-1ba66d146c90
"Enchanted Rock State Natural Area" by Manuel Delgado Tenorio is licensed with CC BY-SA 2.0.
To view a copy of this license, visit https://creativecommons.org/licenses/by-sa/2.0/

The Natural Bridge Caverns in San Antonio
https://search.creativecommons.org/photos/399949b0-d2a2-48e3-bba2-6a7b8abb3956
"natural bridges cavern cave stalagmites stalactites near san antonio texas" by Tim Pearce, Los
Gatos is licensed with CC BY 2.0. To view a copy of this license, visit
https://creativecommons.org/licenses/by/2.0/

Lost Maples State Natural Area
https://search.creativecommons.org/photos/185b7dfb-77fe-462d-a97c-451bc7c6b283
"Lost Maples State Park ,Texas" by VSmithUK is licensed with CC BY 2.0. To view a copy of this license, visit https://creativecommons.org/licenses/by/2.0/

Caddo Lake State Park
https://search.creativecommons.org/photos/1a631ea6-46c9-487e-a6d7-d0d0c8197250
"Caddo Lake State Park" by dustin.askins is licensed with CC BY 2.0. To view a copy of this license, visit https://creativecommons.org/licenses/by/2.0/

Davy Crockett National Forest
https://search.creativecommons.org/photos/ada9a352-bc7b-42e0-820d-89043ea9e43c
"Lake Ratcliff Recreation Area - Davy Crockett National Forest" by Adrian Delgado2012 is licensed with CC BY 2.0. To view a copy of this license, visit https://creativecommons.org/licenses/by/2.0/

Padre Island National Seashore
https://search.creativecommons.org/photos/60ab8eda-4f76-4132-b631-1bf43f36dab0
"Padre Island National Seashore" by National Park Service is marked under CC PDM 1.0. To view the terms, visit https://creativecommons.org/publicdomain/mark/1.0/

Rio Grande Valley
https://search.creativecommons.org/photos/860f7443-851f-45ea-a532-18172bad2412
"Bentsen-Rio Grande Valley State Park, Texas" by VSmithUK is licensed with CC BY 2.0. To view a copy of this license, visit https://creativecommons.org/licenses/by/2.0/

Monahans Sandhills State Park
https://search.creativecommons.org/photos/3e2ee88d-9bc1-451b-9d88-9fdda1cffe35
"Monahans Sandhills State Park" by Plum109 is licensed with CC BY 2.0. To view a copy of this license, visit https://creativecommons.org/licenses/by/2.0/

Seminole Canyon State Park
https://search.creativecommons.org/photos/71708bef-fc5f-480f-b3a7-9908cc78daa8
"Seminole Canyon State Park - White Shaman Tour"by runarut is licensed with CC BY 2.0. To view a copy of this license, visit https://creativecommons.org/licenses/by/2.0/

Marfa Lights of Marfa Texas
https://search.creativecommons.org/photos/3bdaccfe-b006-451c-8a21-3eb72043a768
"Marfa Lights Viewing Area" by TexasExplorer98 is licensed with CC BY 2.0. To view a copy of this license, visit https://creativecommons.org/licenses/by/2.0/

Davis Mountains State Park
https://search.creativecommons.org/photos/becd2362-7e06-4676-af6b-ebf02bf5472c
"top of skyline drive, davis mountains state park" by glg61 is licensed with CC BY 2.0. To view a copy of this license, visit https://creativecommons.org/licenses/by/2.0/

Devil's River State Natural Area
https://search.creativecommons.org/photos/7f2b94a3-1ad5-4699-af56-308d71598484
"Devils River State Natural Area, Val Verde County, Texas" by TexasExplorer98 is licensed with CC BY 2.0. To view a copy of this license, visit https://creativecommons.org/licenses/by/2.0/

Medina River
https://search.creativecommons.org/photos/86a87abd-7ed6-4fb9-b7f7-1a7cbe0252b3
"File:The Medina River in Castroville, TX IMG 3243.JPG" by Billy Hathorn is licensed with CC BY-SA 3.0. To view a copy of this license, visit https://creativecommons.org/licenses/by-sa/3.0

Pedernales State Park
https://search.creativecommons.org/photos/233f20ff-96dc-4b4f-8bfe-710f55ec178d
"File:Pedernales Falls State Park.JPG" by Liveon001 ©Travis Witt is licensed with CC BY-SA 3.0. To view a copy of this license, visit https://creativecommons.org/licenses/by-sa/3.0

117

118

Port Aransas Beach
https://search.creativecommons.org/photos/5461cf70-11e8-4ae9-8261-76cf2806d4ef
"Port Aransas beach, TX" by jdeeringdavis is licensed with CC BY 2.0. To view a copy of this license, visit https://creativecommons.org/licenses/by/2.0/

Rockport Beach
https://search.creativecommons.org/photos/630fb727-7c0e-4de3-9621-733f7d3ca4af
"View From Rockport Beach" by Matthew Oliphant is licensed with CC BY-ND 2.0. To view a copy of this license, visit https://creativecommons.org/licenses/by-nd/2.0/

Seawall Urban Park
https://search.creativecommons.org/photos/88cfb4d9-66a4-41d4-af12-eab0a9bc7183
"Pleasure Pier in Galveston Texas Blue Hour HDR" by Katie Haugland Bowen is licensed with CC BY 2.0. To view a copy of this license, visit https://creativecommons.org/licenses/by/2.0/

South Padre Beach
https://search.creativecommons.org/photos/5f7658f0-1802-47f3-b4cf-cf6a1bc4e911
"South Padre Beach 4" by StuSeeger is licensed with CC BY 2.0. To view a copy of this license, visit https://creativecommons.org/licenses/by/2.0/

Surfside Beach
https://search.creativecommons.org/photos/dff5f3cc-8acf-40d5-9253-beec4415844f
"Surfside Beach, Texas" by big mike - DC is licensed with CC BY 2.0. To view a copy of this license, visit https://creativecommons.org/licenses/by/2.0/

Westcave Waterfalls
https://search.creativecommons.org/photos/457f20c5-654c-4145-82f2-2f785dfea59a
"IMG_0271" by Caleb Feese is licensed with CC BY 2.0. To view a copy of this license, visit https://creativecommons.org/licenses/by/2.0/

Capote Falls
https://www.pinterest.com/pin/516647388483148158/
Bolden, J. A. (n.d.). Capote Falls, West Texas. 1920. Pinterest.
https://www.pinterest.com/pin/516647388483148158/.

Gorman Falls
https://search.creativecommons.org/photos/40261ed8-4160-455a-beb3-bd196075ffb5
"Gorman Falls, Texas" by Tracy Keller is licensed with CC BY-SA 2.0. To view a copy of this license, visit https://creativecommons.org/licenses/by-sa/2.0/

Cattails Falls
https://search.creativecommons.org/photos/b191b4e3-0c0b-498b-993b-a0a5d5ff2367
"cattail-falls" by rezendi is licensed with CC BY 2.0. To view a copy of this license, visit https://creativecommons.org/licenses/by/2.0/

Dolan Falls
https://search.creativecommons.org/photos/8e26f8fd-3ba9-48ea-aa0e-86169c300439
"File:Devils River - Dolan Falls (174119624).jpg" by Clinton & Charles Robertson from RAF Lakenheath, UK & San Marcos, TX, USA & UK is licensed with CC BY-SA 2.0. To view a copy of this license, visit https://creativecommons.org/licenses/by-sa/2.0

Boykin Springs
https://search.creativecommons.org/photos/35f9ca95-72fd-4df5-8d6a-9332f8c95bbf
"Boykin Springs bridge" by US Forest Service - Southern Region is licensed with CC BY-SA 2.0. To view a copy of this license, visit https://creativecommons.org/licenses/by-sa/2.0/

Waco Mammoth National Monument
https://search.creativecommons.org/photos/1c934de6-a323-4e0a-8b43-5f9719cdf850
"File:Waco mammoth site QRT.jpg" by Larry D. Moore is licensed with CC BY-SA 3.0. To view a copy of this license, visit https://creativecommons.org/licenses/by-sa/3.0

Big Thicket Natural Preserve
https://search.creativecommons.org/photos/b5c1492c-fcaa-43d7-a1ed-bdd60d6f45b5
"20120106-OC-AMW-0698" by USDAgov is marked under CC PDM 1.0. To view the terms, visit
https://creativecommons.org/publicdomain/mark/1.0/

Lake Conroe
https://search.creativecommons.org/photos/39c9d66e-159e-4efa-bf1b-b9ac67b42292
"Lake Conroe" by eng1ne is licensed with CC BY 2.0. To view a copy of this license, visit
https://creativecommons.org/licenses/by/2.0/

Lake Bob Sandlin
https://www.shutterstock.com/image-photo/lakeside-living-128350181
Sheridan, B. (n.d.). Lakeside Living. Shutterstock. https://www.shutterstock.com/image-photo/lakeside-living-128350181.

Lake Fork
https://search.creativecommons.org/photos/8a495d6e-d237-4d54-85e0-414491ecbf3c
"Sunset over Lake Fork" by Tammy McGary is licensed under CC BY 2.0

Cover photo: https://unsplash.com/photos/03mmXv9INVI
Thomas Brushel – Photographer

Made in the USA
Coppell, TX
12 December 2021